ALEKSANDR ORLOV

PRESENTS

Bogdan

& THE BIG RACE

**MEERKAT
CLASSICS**

RUSSIA 2012

Bogdan & the Big Race
ALEKSANDR ORLOV

1 3 5 7 9 10 8 6 4 2

First published in 2012 by Ebury Press, an imprint of Ebury Publishing

A Random House Group company

The Random House Group Limited Reg. No. 954009

Addresses for companies within the Random House Group can be found at
www.randomhouse.co.uk

A CIP catalogue record for this book is available from the British Library

The Random House Group Limited supports The Forest Stewardship Council
(FSC®), the leading international forest certification organisation. Our
books carrying the FSC label are printed on FSC® certified paper. FSC is
the only forest certification scheme endorsed by the leading environmental
organisations, including Greenpeace. Our paper procurement policy can be
found at www.randomhouse.co.uk/environment

Printed and bound in Italy by Graphicom SRL

ISBN 9780091950033

To buy books by your favourite authors and register for offers visit
www.randomhouse.co.uk

A MESSAGE FROM THE AUTHOR

Hello peoples of UK!

Welcome to another storytelling from Meerkovo. This time we are teaching you how do to arithmetics. Only jokings! Actually we are telling you a tale of great derring-do.

When you read this story of furry-braveness, we hope that you feel a throb of excitement. Because if you are young and small, like hero of this book, you don't always know that you are being taken serious. (Especially if like little Bogdan you are famous for your practical jokings). But if you try very, very hard you will be taken serious and then you can winnings.

My Great Granddaddy Vitaly was always tell me that winnings isn't as important as the playings. Personally I think it is good to both.

Please enjoyment.

Yours,

Aleksandr

ALEKSANDR ORLOV

It was **beautiful** sunny day.

All the meerkats of Meerkovo have their sun creams on.
Some of them are wearing sunglasses on their noses.
(If you have not seen meerkats with sunglasses on,
then you are not lookings hard enough).

It was the kind of day when a meerpup who has day
off school feels happy to be alive.

For this is very specials day. It is the final of the

Meerkovian Grand Prix

– the biggest race in all the Russia.
Every famous driver and all the
fastest cars are gathering
together to find out who
is Champion of
Champions.

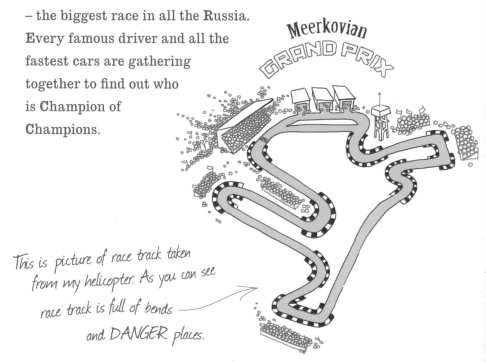

This is picture of race track taken
from my helicopter. As you can see
race track is full of bends
and DANGER places.

The crowd is full of cheering meerpups and their mothers and fathers. Everyone has their packed weevil and termite lunch.* There is excitements everywhere.

On one side of track is villagers of Meerkovo. They are waving special flags that have been claw-stitched by Sergei. (He stayed up all night to make. Which made him very tired and moulty).

On other side of track are the **stinky mongooses.** All the meerkats keep well away from them. As any meerpup will tell you, mongooses are scratchy and full of meanness, and they are the enemy.

*This is very popular Meerkovo snack. It is full of nourishings and is good for thick fur and happy disposition.

Neeeeeeeeeeeaow!*

One by one the cars get behind starting line. Big roar go up.

They are off! **"They're off!"** shout the crowd.
All the cars are painted brightly and look sparkle in the sunshine.

*Neeeeeeeeeeeaow!** They go.

Everyone cheered. "Hurrah," they shout. And, just to make sure, "Hurray".

Round corner comes blue car. Then green one, and then yellow one. "All the colours of the rainbow," says wise old meerkat in commentary box. (He is very old and has done many commenting. He always say this about the rainbows).

*You must read this very noisily.
Racing cars are always noise.

Then come **mysterious red car.**

It is sleek and very fast. It makes roar so mighty the crowd cannot hear itself think. It edge past green car. Then the yellow one. Then it was just behind the blue car.

The crowd gasp and grip the edge of its seat. Who is this mystery driver who is so skill and brave? Nobody know. It is all very puzzlement.

Mystery red car has extra big pipes and number one on it. But otherwise it is typical ultra-modern racing car.

Just then it overtake blue car and is in the lead.

"He is making all the other drivers eat his dust," says wise old meerkat in commentary box.

He is always talking about the dust as well. (Perhaps this is because he is a very dusty wise old meerkat).

Then up goes a shout. **"It's Bogdan!"** It is!

Meerkovo's favourite meerpup. (Despite his prankings, peoples still find him adorables). Everyone jumps up and down in excitements.

Even old Grigor is bouncing up and down in his wheelchair. (Or perhaps he is just forgetting to take his medications).

Then right behind Bogdan's car comes car with big black smoke.

It has evil written all over it.*

*This is a figure of speeches. It does not mean 'evil' was actually written on the car. It mean the car was all nastiness and horridness.

It has push its nose past the yellow and the green
and the blue car until it is just behind the red car.

It is driven by big hairy mongoose who look wicked and
rotten and full of nastiness. He tries to pass Bogdan's
red car but Bogdan too fast.

He try again and even clip wing of
Bogdan's car. Still Bogdan stay ahead.
Then evil mongoose start to play dirty.
He flick a switch and suddenly

spikes come out of his wheels!

The crowd gasp. This is all
very frightenings.

The mongoose come up behind Bogdan

and make his spikes cut into his car.

The crowd now shout and scream in great alarmings,

But somehow Bogdan manage to keep on track.

Then the dirty mongoose make another attack.

This time Bogdan sees it coming and he swerve out of way at last minute. The mongoose car goes flying past and goes straight into barriers.

Big swirly smoke billows out of his car.

The crowd could see the mongoose hopping up and down in a rage and a furiousness.

CRASH!

Meanwhile, the red car zoom on to the finishing line. It is way ahead of all other cars.

The chequeredy flag come down with big flourish.

Bogdan is first!

He is winning by 5.5 seconds!

The crowd is beside itself with delightedness.

This diagram reveals secret behind success chequeredy flag-waving. It may look simples, but actually require great skill.

Bogdan is hero!

He climb out of cockpit and is immediately surround by cheering fans.

The race director takes him by the paw and guides him to podium.

There the President of all the Russias congratulate him and hang big medal round his neck. The brass band play Meerkovo Anthem – which is very rousing, and makes the crowd very rouse.

It was wonderful. Bogdan had never feel so proud. (He is sometimes naughty pup, and is no stranger to the dunce's cap, so it is very good for him to be achieving). He could see his mother and father and all his brothers and sisters jumping up and down in the crowd.

Presidents is hold medal ready for presentation. ──────▶
It is built to giant scale and so heavy
I think he is worry he drop it!

There was **Miss Maiya** his teacher. There was **Vassily**

Miss Maiya

Vassily

and **Great Uncle Grigor.** There was **Sergei** in the pits.

And there was...

Great Uncle Grigor

Sergei

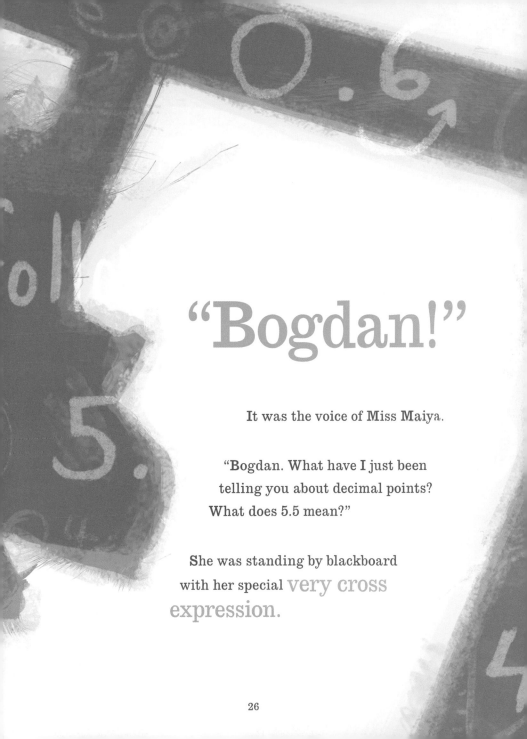

"Bogdan!"

It was the voice of Miss Maiya.

"Bogdan. What have I just been
telling you about decimal points?
What does 5.5 mean?"

She was standing by blackboard
with her special very cross
expression.

Bogdan gulped.

He clutched his gleaming red toy car (it was **Yakov's** finest, and was present from his **Great Uncle Grigor**) and gaze at Miss Maiya. He knows he ought to know about decimal points, somehow he knows it will be important to know one day.

I'm afraid this is not the exercise book of a hard-working pup. He should be writing equations and not illustrating himself.

But just at that moment it isn't mattering. It may have been a dream, and he may be going straight to the detention, but Bogdan now know what he is going to be when he grew up: the fastest racing driver in the whole universe.

Aleksandr's Life Lesson

You must climb every rainbow to make your dreams come true.

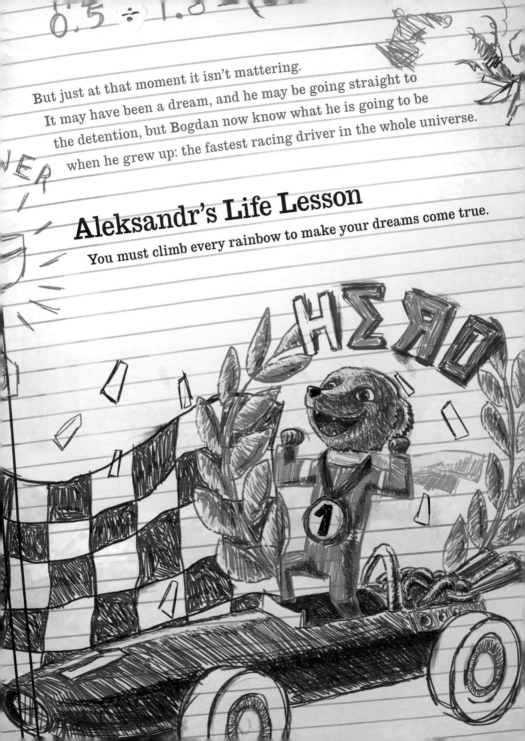

Now read my other greatest tales

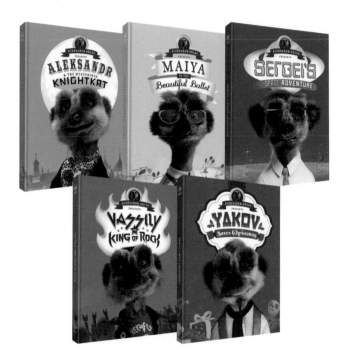

Available from all good bookshops

Also available to download as an ebookamabob
or audiomajig as read by the author – me!

For more information visit www.comparethemeerkat.com

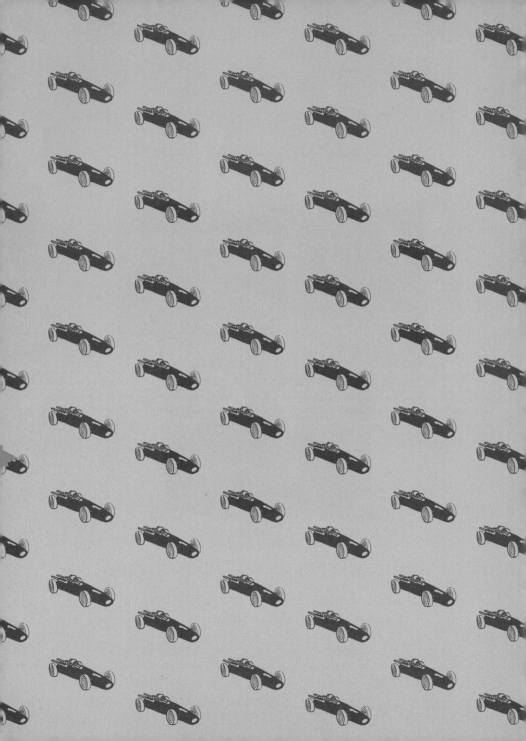